Silk Purses and Lemonade

poems by

Elizabeth Robin

Finishing Line Press
Georgetown, Kentucky

Silk Purses and Lemonade

Copyright © 2017 by Elizabeth Robin
ISBN 978-1-63534-173-7 First Edition
All rights reserved under International and Pan-American Copyright Conventions.
No part of this book may be reproduced in any manner whatsoever without written permission from the publisher, except in the case of brief quotations embodied in critical articles and reviews.

ACKNOWLEDGMENTS

Thank you to the following publications in which these poems first appeared, some in slightly different form:

"A Netherworld" *Autumn Sky Poetry Daily*
"Deus ex Machina," "The Problem with Words," and "Truth or Dare" *I am not a silent poet*
"All-American Meme" *Hilton Head Island: Time and Tide*, an anthology of the Island Writers' Network
"A Simple Pleasure" *Life on the May*

A big island thanks, y'all, to the Island Writers' Network, to Reuben Wooley, editor of I am not a silent poet and Curly Mind, and to the talented Mira Scott, for the encouragement and inspiration.
To Brandon, Lauren, and Amanda, with love always.
To Jeanne, who trusted both love and swans would return.
To Russell, who never believed in flying pigs, only Hail Mary passes.
And to my dear George, who saw flying pigs everywhere. Bonsai. I will find you where green meets blue.

Publisher: Leah Maines

Editor: Christen Kincaid

Cover Art: Danielle Klim

Author Photo: Cara McNeil Donoghue

Cover Design: Elizabeth Maines

Printed in the USA on acid-free paper.
Order online: www.finishinglinepress.com
also available on amazon.com

Author inquiries and mail orders:
Finishing Line Press
P. O. Box 1626
Georgetown, Kentucky 40324
U. S. A.

Table of Contents

Stuck 1
A Netherworld 2
Silk Purses 3
Deus Ex Machina 4
Truth, or Dare? 6
All-American Meme 7
Mislaid Glory 8
The Problem with Words 9
The Invisible Wall 11
American Standard 12
Mira's World 13
Under a New Jersey Moon 14
Santa Fe in Layers 16
Lemonade 17
Fashionation 18
The Denizens of St. Lawrence Gap 19
A Simple Pleasure 20
Synchrony 21
Waiting 22
Magic Lanterns 23
Beware of Flying Pigs 24
The Mystic Knot 25
Biohazards 26
Telemetry 27
Step into my Arcade 29
Bonsai 31

Stuck

I used to watch the raindrops trickle
across the window, making shapes
and tracks as we travelled the Alps

or schlepped to school. The hours spent
studying each tiny sphere, its motion
squiggling diagonally across the glass
in mini-jumps, its lifespan fitting neatly
the length of that rear window.

How much of my childhood I spent
watching, listening, feeling, waiting!

I'd sit and study an ant as it hauled
some cargo back to somewhere,
its purpose hidden but compelling.

I'd stare at waves folding onto a rocky
Capri shore, the crystalline teal water
mesmerizing, a warm and salty tang.

I'd cluster with the neighborhood pack
and roam from sledding hill to corner grocer
collecting bubblegum and Topps cards.

Now I scurry in a mindless triptych
to vacuous or unfulfilled destinations,
our front yards and parks emptied,
endless-inning pick-up games as lost as that one
stubborn raindrop that clings to the far corner,
quivering, shaken, yet refusing to move.

A Netherworld

From the frosted glass emerges a figure—
slim, quixotic in posture—with a giant
schlong ending at knees created by
trickling drops. Fertility figures

must quiver, cast sidelong glances
from their appointed Met displays.
Labeled merely "wood: Igbo" masks
the clues that narrow place and tribe.
teak? mahogany? ebony? mango?

Identity matters, she thinks, as water
slides down the shower wall, erasing
her Bangwa king, the steamy replica
her imagination conjures in a misty stall.

The crude, oversized, exaggerated hope
worries at her fevered mind. What next?
Jesus in honeyed pancakes?
Buddha in the laundry pile?

Silk Purses

maybe if i shave my legs spring will come

i daintily side-step around my confusion
i climb through the blurred, darkened opening

eating words for breakfast, the edges of my mind
feel sharpened, like a ribbon-shredding oyster shell
awake, I realize my facelessness

maybe he's in Carsland, driving
through jaw-dropping redrock cliffs—
or Dismaland, where Cinderella crashes

and he burns—or maybe he's still here,
in some alternate plane where leaving
without a word seems civilized, simple, kind

he's still not here: only his ghost in random
misplaced socks, the suit stored in the back closet

i will spin a gossamer sheen of silk, a veil
masking sorrow and joy, build a compact

purse, compress my world to fit inside his
into the eminent domain of spectral territory

i'll open that silk purse and cram it with laughs
stuff in cries until life bursts its cloture
and everything actually has a reason

sand works the oyster and i become the pearl
made by Disney, scripted in Hollywood
a dreamscape approved for mass production

Deus Ex Machina

she climbs, a methodical looping of two separate ropes
intricately attached and wound around the harness
connecting her to the hate-filled pole she scales

voices call from below: *ma'am, come down off the pole*
her chirpy voice saying, *I know sir, I'm prepared*
in reply to some vague, inaudible police statement

the pole shakes with each increment she advances
as quiet surrounds a statehouse in acquiescence
to a symbol fixed by their law: no half-mast here

come against me with hatred and violence, she calls
resurrecting visions of Mother Emanuel, a bloody history
I come with God, and this flag comes down today

she repeats, *whom shall I fear? whom shall I fear?*
poses for an AP wire photo of racism, unclipped all too briefly
brave words as she rappels to policemen, hands raised

remembering Walter Scott and six burning churches
a KKK resurgence and its special brand of terror
and nine praying, studying words of God, mowed down

their kin, one by one, forgive a tenth, who prayed
in fellowship, then spat out hatred in a hail of bullets
his flag, emblem of that bigotry, flies above their coffins

high and unashamed. governors, legislators, wring hands
hoisted by that petard of a veiled and twisted heritage
on that statehouse post—*and what should we fear?*

a chant begins to smattering applause from a handful
taping for youtube, repeating *we must love and protect
each other, we have nothing to lose but our chains*

we see her, we hear her, thanks to that lone historian,
one cellphone recording a crime and arrest to recitations
the 23rd Psalm, *the Lord is my light* in call and response

echoes across a nation harnessed to that flag, and one woman
brave enough to dismantle our conscience in a precise act
of joyous scripture and civil disobedience, a meticulous
de-facing of the terroristic bigotry woven into stars and bars

Truth, or Dare?

once, prophesies that bearded gods
wear silver brought ruin to the gullible
gold and chocolate to the conquistador

now, rusted grainy metal rises in a sequoian
cylinder above the treeline, dwarfing pines
the toilet brush top garnished in synthetic
prickly green, scrubbing an open blue sky

the monopine dominates, and soon
borders carved in tribal violation
for pots of room service cocoa
unlimited cellphone access
and gated uniformity
render only museum adventures
where native plants and tribes live in diorama
or a gullah cabin restored, a novelty stop
complete with artifact audio tour

and someday, we may wonder what we gain
and what we lose, in our fabrications

All-American Meme

I see an acid-washed Emma Lazarus
at the base of a weeping statue
of a lady in distress

she wields a rolling pin
that flattens a pasty white dough
pushing out, popping errant bubbles
of brown and black and yellow
scattered by her tears

she watches helplessly
as children tumble backward
arms flailing
or handcuffed
palms pressed together
in supplication

new scribbles overlay that iconic poetry
messages of judgment, censure
nationalism, generalization
advertising only white space

the awful blankness on a statuary base
spawns a dead, negative void

a fresh meme for the world-weary
resurrecting the old order

Mislaid Glory

I shake one in each clenched fist,
pom-poms cheering on the parade.

I wear red, white and blue apparel,
a teensy-weensy flag bikini,
or a cape swathed over a tee-shirt
whose iron-on appliqué displays
my superhero-sized Old Glory.

I eat corn ears and smothered hot dogs
off flags in decoupage on TV trays
gaze at a patriotic Jasper Johns
print above the fireplace screen.

I walk past lawns whose borders
flitter mini-flags the entire periphery,
past cars with plastic fluttering antennas,
past bumpers and billboards plastered
with national fervor in stars and stripes.

And I forget about lowering Glory at sunset
or in the rain and snow, and I ask, sharply
"Where's your flag?" and forget,
what lies in two triangular boxes,
precisely folded by an honor guard
rigid with reverence and rules and salutes.

The Problem with Words

stiff, red-splotched men at three-martini
lunches speak in metaphor, their urgency
underscored in ridicule—negotiation,
compromise show weakness—
they call for boots, boots, boots on the ground

i despise synecdoche that shapes horror.
are there words to squelch canned movie lines
rolled out replaying a game little boys extend
from their cowboy-and-indian days?

who wears these boots, sent to some extreme
and alien climate, brought to harsh tests packed
with rules unwritten, or in some alien tongue?

ask for boots, boots, boots on the ground
and betray those thousands we bury
or ignore in VA hospitals and mental wards

while hungry tongues lap up war and swallow
drones, snipers, bombers-most-Christian,
market collateral damage in flippant phrases
tossed out like candy to greedy warmongers

call them boots
but don't pretend
what we risk
is just a little leather
and some laces

end these little euphemisms and stomach the truth:
we memorialize dead boots but rarely support the living
ask them to kill and destroy, send our children
our brothers and sisters, our husbands and wives
to witness atrocity that ruins their psyches
leaves them homeless, in despair, suicidal
in an endless loop of paperwork and pain
for boots, boots, boots and more boots

while those rigid old hawks
in polished wing-tipped oxfords
rake in their cut of the profits
spreading their oily words

The Invisible Wall

although undetectable
a Wonder Woman in her jet plane
flies without the lasso to rappel up and away
from the ever-tightening noose
of loving expectations

the DC Comic world offers
cool invisibility
a special power, often heroically applied

but here, rendered inconsequential
like yesterday's veil
pummeled into obsolescence
or worse, pinched and squelched
into the oblivion of the no call list

I still look great in my star-studded
red white and blue
even though an imperceptible wall
barricades the world
from my intrusion

American Standard

some scripts fit predictable patterns
and a well-worn cast of characters

in film noire a blankness lurks
threatens a tangible, peripheral evil

the woman, alluring yet distant
offers jaunty comebacks
but freezes at danger
can only scream silently
and stagger back in stilettos

stalked and held at whim
she plays the victim
and not just in movies

leave him and hope
he's not flush with his right
to ownership

or, that when she's found
some salty gumshoe
can scrape the evidence
from her broken
and bloody fingernails

Mira's World
Inspired by artist Mira Scott's painting "The Sacred Mushroom"

overlarge, bulbous and bright red
sturdy stem fringed by a matching tutu
eerily down and center-stage, in Mira's world
a sacred mushroom transcends time and space
into a polka dot suite of acid-dropping color

and a time teeming turtles and frogs and snails
ladybugs and garter snakes and dragonflies
where mushrooms are still holy
and vibrant flowers enfold precious eggs
turtles flock to the blue swirling waters
statuesque pines shade and tower
and brace the osprey's aerie

set back, miniaturized and benign
a handful of cottages offer stewardship
and wonder, at the magic of Mira's world
where honeybees and monarchs flit inside
and between and around her wrinkle in time

infuse smoke and toxins and waste
abuse the indigenous for the convenient
be the pirate of neutrals and destruction

and miss Mira's world

a place transfixed in wild ginger
and fiddlehead fern
and blossom after blossom
beauty at once divine and fundamental
a Love Island of rejuvenation and abundance

after the snowmelt
move back, back, and back again
and worship at the altar
of Mira's world

Under a New Jersey Moon

This morning I counted the swans in the lake
in honor of Margaret Jeanne: fourteen scattered
in languid pairs, heads dipping elegantly down
butts popping up, as if mooning New Jersey.

This is no bucolic getaway
but a last chip of peeled paint
that vestige of old Lake of the Lilies where once
thousands of blooming pads covered her waters
after the lilies die
after the dunes breech
after all reeds are razed, buffers gone
testament to expert landscapers
and density building.

A plane of flattened, spoon-shaped cotton disks
stretch out beyond the water tower, sharp edges
drawn against a bright noon sky; silence lulls through
midday doldrums, sun and heat languishing as sirens
helicopters and train whistles pierce the calm.

Banners streak out behind struggling single engines
announcing the latest happy hour deal
or vodka brand *du jour*. Cars stream down the shore
packing thirty dollar day lots and tacky arcades.

Bennies and Canadian geese mass upon each square
inch of sand and lake; excrement and loud squawking
fill the million dollar view, a puddle packed with displaced
ocean sand, geese and people that forgot to go home.

Everything's confused, and the dune line
—well that's a highway now. I hear in winter
the lake froze solid, a shortcut to the grocer's,
and pickup hockey games or amateur skaters

swarmed to the launch spot now fenced
for the property owners association.

The willow trees went in ninety-seven
and each year I watch another chestnut die
or oak disappear. Swans and little cygnets,
ducks and ducklings swim in military precision
pecking order complete, behind proud mamas.

Now there are eighteen. The afternoon sunlight
dances in twinkles and ripples of soft wind,
glances in flirty winks and caresses.
Reflections—both abutting houses and wistful musings
glitter up, mirroring what greeted Margaret Jeanne
sipping coffee on her back porch.

On our last morning there were a dozen swans—
and buzzing, the hum of clear-cutting nest reeds
and a mist so fine it blurred the treeless sardine homes
and a lake fringe razed to ground zero.

The links are off a rusted chain; there's nothing
to eat the mice, and a Jersey lake runs a war
of attrition. The hawks and snakes have left,
and the home saved from two storms
of the century cannot weather overrunning vermin
nor another lot opened to emptiness and clear-cutting—
turtles dry, and ducks and swans nest in concrete.

I can see Jeanne's glee, as the clouds cover a harvest moon
in wispy strips. I count sixteen swans now, always
an even number. She smiled: "They mate for life."

Perhaps that's why the moon veils itself, the sweet
sixteen pumping by, glaring at the bare shoreline.

Santa Fe in Layers

we live in a concrete house, where the land is harsh
and welcoming, and shady cottonwood trees snow
across highways with travel plaza casinos and unmarked exits
fortunes for a quarter in a lost expanse of neon mesquite and dry air

sunbaked riverbeds run dogs and serial walkers
energized by rolled oats and brown
sugar bars made with Santa Fe love
home to Georgia and George RR, strata variegate from pale
rose to iron-red, pink almond blooms and brush
in icy blue-tinged or shocking yellow-veined greens
canyons, houses, flower beds, all mired
in the blush and orange adobe clay

a native passes in a REDSKIN tee shirt
nods hello, smiles at the ironic
ownership he markets

mountains flatten into mesas miles long
whitewater rafters dare the rushing Rio Grande
and ghost ranches tell tales of fratricide, cattle
rustled and vaqueros robbed, their buried gold
revealed by escaping widows crossing arroyos
with children in the night of a wild west flash
flood with epic lightening, washes instantly soaked
and drained, like one ranch owner whose wife
signed a deed one day, divorced him the next

wilderness and opportunity so often commingle

Lemonade

the jackhammer seldom sleeps next door
refrains from coffee breaks, an early lunch
its rattle-trapping mars clear thinking

keep pedaling that bicycle or fall down
inertia can be a powerful force through
both joyful and damaging distractions

the woodpecker tock-tock-tock, squirrel vibrato
cricket chirps and frog riddits, flitter
through consciousness, inspire and calm

but like trampled shrubbery, what decorated
becomes the eyesore—these bursts shatter stillness
chinoiserie quivers, once-secure floating shelves

now wall-surfing as constant battering rouses
all, agitated until consciousness pains
consumes, absorbs, obliterates both concrete

and creativity: a man crept into my poem
unannounced. perhaps he seeps from the closet
urn, or shakes through reverberating walls

squeeze lemons! make lemonade! pour out
a pitcher of sweet and sour joy. i remember
the glass and its cascading lemonfall flows

Fashionation

I spot a woman driving, her face
covered by gigantic oval sunglasses.
Immense flowers cover her bigshirt.
A neon straw hat clashes with that majestic
floral design. I recognize the type, of an age
she's gone from fashionista to middle finger salute.

Much like that little girl twirling in her yard
in royal blue stars, pastel plaid, striped socks—
a gleeful uncaring skip through style,
runaway with childhood whims,
color, bling and glitter shoes.

They meet, and fall into magical stories
of elves and faeries from faraway worlds
conspirators peering through a lens
carefree, and packed with bubble-chasing.

Her mum and dad work in shades of charcoal
black and blue. Suburban wife and teen march
in uniform jean-and-tee, fit a form
as seen in cosmo, elle or vogue,
monochrome restricted by the latest
must-have, the newest must-wear, photoshopped
to skeletal fashionation. Sameness flourishes.

Why lose those days when dancing iridescent globes,
opaque prisms of light and joy, blow for breezes to catch
and chase, a game where little gigglers race, nab, pop,
bring tingling laughter—and any outfit will do?

I will scrub my face clean. Or slap on bright cherry red
or lime crime serpentina apocalipstick
and a broad-brimmed crazy hat, dance a tango
in backless chiffon or batik muumuu,
and follow those bubbles bouncing in the wind.

The Denizens of St. Lawrence Gap

i cast about for clues in the walleyed man
his plaid long-sleeves, in burning humidity,
clash with floral bermudas. ankle-length dreads
baffle. how old he must be, hair locked in what
decade of languidness? i dodge his white cane.

young men haunt sidewalks
step in time, or form a gauntlet
of eyes and clarion calls
that force speed-walk scuttles
back to compound walls

a guard sits at the back entrance, fresh paint
and solid concrete mark his gatehouse. furnished
with a single chair, he rarely glances up

beach entrepreneurs hawk jewels from little attachés
beads and bangles, shells and sailing expeditions

restaurant owners glad-hand passersby, soapbox
a menu at rude boyz jerk kitchen, or rush to unfurl
awnings to keep the harlequin tables dry

i step over or around or through vacant eyes
and outstretched hands. is it a pretense? a belief
he's not really blind? a ruse those rags dress
for beggars' parts? what am i, shopping for baubles
while he accepts bakery crumbs and cast offs?

A Simple Pleasure

today i found that sock
the one that disappeared in the laundry months ago
the one i sifted and sorted and searched to recover
the one that was cushy and fuzzy and warm
the one that brought piggly wiggly joy

reunited with its lonely mate
the one who's been waiting, alone in that dark cold drawer
abandoned twin haunting the sock section—
so patient, trusting her match would return some day—
taunting my helplessness, my haphazard wardrobe control

and just when i'd abandoned all hope, there, just there
inside the form-fitting folds of last season's sheets
there, yes there, better than graduation and trophies
and christmas morning
euphoria, because today
i found that sock

Synchrony

a speckled red-footed pigeon pecks
through legs, under a maze of eyes
undetected by those glued to palm
sized screens, thumbing intel, mired
in toys like toddlers in parallel play
each positioned in virtual synchronicity
leaning forward, faces aglow, eyes dull

i can go anywhere in the world
and live the same experience
munching custom burgers, visiting
the riviera and food court heaven

like mosquitos buzzing, they repeat
hash tags from quotable quotes, preach
redundancy without roots or leaves

a couple argues, hugs, then resumes
an awkward and public courtship
needy clinging, sound-effect kisses
flamboyant stage embraces
visible from the mezzanine—
just as flying ants swarm,
only the fastest males mate

connections depend on device or theater
innovation morphs into novelty
says the film museum curator

dulled by cacophony
he laughs and laughs

Waiting

life pressed on pause
time stretched between one place
and another, one person
or another, until moments interstice
a world of stranger seats
newslessness, a void of nonevents
quiet contemplation

waiting
can be emptying

screen addicts and button pushers
meet players on the prowl
raking clothes off
with vulture eyes

waiting
can be uncomfortable

ear buds drown
the white noise of inanity
talking expands, fills the space
presses out thoughts

waiting
can be deafening

in locations marked by crowd garbage
and overused toilets, vistas of sameness
metal and concrete without beauty
or utility or imagination

waiting
can be windowless

a soul-closing vacuum
back to a life

Magic Lanterns

an Edwardian attic in Winterbourne tells a regressive story
displays the roomful of cots and dollhouses, wooden minicarts
and iron pennybanks, an array of magic lanterns lighting
a new age of industry and vitality. starched little shirtfronts
and christening gowns stuffing massive chiffarobes that venture
downstairs as its charges assume their rightful stewardship
over the largest screw, nut and bolt factory in the world

and down the hall a small anteroom lies
its one narrow iron bed, sensible
wardrobe, window to a front garden
she sees, but cannot share nor till
an in-between, closeted in her study
that is dining hall and sleeping quarters—
the governess took her meals here alone, reads
the placard, *her station exceeding the help
yet below the children she schooled*

down the road sits blue collar utopia in Bourneville
a social experiment in open space communal living
testament to forward thinking industrialists
miracle of urban planning
offering affordable housing and family fun

yet their teachers and nursemaids
laying the foundation for their children
access no park or community picnic
receive no musicale or dinner invites
enjoy no magic lantern filmfests
but walk alone, eat alone, converse
only to the walls of this multi-functional space

a lifetime avocation pasted in free time
and the joy of solitary confinement

Beware of Flying Pigs

Retreat into a downy cocoon,
insulated in sleep.
A choice.

Babble unending platitudes
masked as deep philosophical truths,
absorbed by words vomiting pain.
Another option.

Check on everyone's wellbeing
but your own. Gulp down angst
like a nestling at its first meal,
choking on possibility.

Distract with pounding repetition.
Resurrection myths, snake oil remedies . . .
Each method offers its own brand of hope.

I filter walking along a shore,
where meaning lies within each tidal change.

He stands like Custer, unbending,
angry others retreat into statistical impossibility.
"When pigs fly," he shouts.
"That's when I'll give up."

Shamed by his confidence,
I retract inside a cynic's shell
and respond, "Beware of flying pigs."

The Mystic Knot

the ties no longer bind
thus says the dominatrix
in her cold, clipped note
before the corpse cools

our galvanized chain link fences
forge a mirage of neighborly ephemera

friends won and lost by clicking
a box with a mouse, and scores
settled with displaced aggression
mass shootings or self-immolation
address books bare rubbed erasures
and a history of scrub-a-dub liaisons

when life's affirmed by crowdfunding
rather than tenderness
and funereal ribbons thread
cornucopias of regret
called gift baskets
Sancho Panza becomes Iago
longing for a pillow or a rope

mystic knots protect no one
wealth, everlasting love
end. we miss a beginning
or an ending, knotting time
interlocking spirits

but the charm of longevity
just another relic, dissolved
like trust, loyalty, devotion
yet another lie from the mist

Biohazards

barnacles seem
                too permanent
                              too clingy

create an endless drydock life
hitchhike on a back for years
glue in until fixed to our very scars

some imagine a life barely tethered
land, obligations dissolving
rollicking seascapes hopping
one pirate vessel
                or another

they chisel and scrape and sand furiously at old hulls
revarnish surfaces
but scars last for decades
their removal requires toxic pollutants

deter attachments with biohazards
and set sail across hazardous shoals
lured by rogue waves and ignore
one scientific marvel

even barnacles have doors
                      that open
                          or close

Telemetry

in a dustless vacuum
starchy-clean uniforms check
a series of beeps and blips
pumps and drips

alien machines dictate heartbeat and breath
the barely discernible swathed figure
fully tubed and automated
thrives by telemetry

poets imagine they sabotage
such revisions of mortality,
shape questions in meter, diction,
clever metaphor—synecdoche, even—

do they differ from those doctors
who diagnose intake and outflow
calibrated in milliliters?

measure for measure we quantify life
á tempo, the final stanza, certain

rhythms noted in tones and graphs
betray the lie in telemetry: life
palliates no one's hope
that probes and gadgets
procedures and exploits
alter our fate

tilers mark off square footage
calculated to the last ceramic inch
but artists who paint by numbers
rarely hang in the Louvre

that customized frame
may surround a masterpiece
but only a woman's enigmatic smile
illumines the mystery of human will

as scientists analyze beakers and formulas
find statistical significance in measured results—
and governments rely upon speed limits, opinion polls,
and clean checkmarks in neat application boxes—
we remain confounded by the caldera faith refutes,
the joy one thin beam of sunlight brings a room,
the unabashed awe in a moment captured on a Sistine ceiling
the majesty of a mountain vista, or a newborn child

a shimmering mirage, this comfort
in electronic light and sound
a tactility confirming presence
that only a living will denies

yes, telemetry may be a lie
but the poet's schemata
the tragedian's catharsis
that rule of law, the slide specimen data
no matter the mark, all manipulate
a concerto of bafflement

melodic movements
to our transitoriness

Step into my Arcade

The training wheels are off—
I am the last one breathing

I am a pachinko ball rolling through a perpetual
staircase of tessellating family portraits
iterations of abandonment that continually morph
into another version of the past.

Dreams and reality blend in a mind
as sharp and complicated as a Chopin etude
fumbled fingering stumbling along keys
tricky to read, trickier to process.

Mosaics of lives pieced, pulled up
signs they ever existed, erased.

I am a cross between Jackie O
and Audrey, an interlocking Warhol
reiterating old lessons—
what nice girls don't do
what others miss when they don't value me
what toughlove helps me endure.

Kiss and Go, Kiss and Go

I am John Wayne, only tougher
nose permanently skewed sideways
I tell no tales, I just abide
retell the pragmatism in budgets
and tackling tragedy in single steps.

Kiss and Go, Kiss and Go

I am Adonis, Golden Boy in black and white
a Brownie camera checkerboard so idyllic
I'm the ever-burning star, shining;
my entourage clings as I cinder
into a shattering supernova.

Kiss and Go, Kiss and Go

In the constancy of self-inflicted wounds
treading means surviving, but not living.

I am not afraid. I cascade down a forest
then up among stars that percolate across
memories confirming they lived, loved
me. Heresy, fifty years of conversations
with myself, to myself, keeping her alive.

Kiss and Go. Kiss. And Go.

An escape from casual water can be deep—
even this pachinko ball can be lost
in love's gamble. Kiss. And Go.

We make things obtuse in our struggle—
even our games are so lonely, so serious.
But death is rarely trivial, and desertion
a hollow escape. Pachinko balls drop
through those moments we ache,
reminding us, always, kiss, and go.

Bonsai

winter's a poor time to become a widow
like the bonsai, i writhe through a universe
contained and minitiarized, snipped and shaped
with brass wires and bamboo twists
left on a cold windowsill shrinking
into grotesques, a rendering down

i marvel. they see a bonsai's deformity
as art, label it sacred—a transformed treasure
revere the *wabi-sabi* in patina and weathering
celebrate flaws, mend fissures with gold filament

but no gold fills this cracking canyon

i yearn to jump beyond planetary limits
and find a practical purpose past
yoga poses and window dressing

trees should touch the sky, swaying shade cloaking
clandestine rendezvous, a bower for tempestuous trysts
left untampered, stretching beyond horizons

i cultivate tray playthings for cures, pursue
a meaning above re-creation and magic
where it's not too late for tigers or elephants
or him, and smallness feels holy

i replicate memories inside a newly flattened bowl
seeking the conduit to charm spring blossoms
that bolt me beyond the moon

Elizabeth Robin retired to Hilton Head Island after a 33-year teaching career to devote herself to writing. She began with *Becoming Mrs. L*, a still unpublished teaching memoir. She started a children's book series; *Gracie Learns English* and *Gracie's Secret World* currently seek a publisher. Then she found poetry as a response and outlet to a fresh grief, watching her brother battle acute myeloid leukemia for 27 months. Her first poem, "A Lowcountry Path" was published in a local magazine January, 2015.

A poet of witness and discovery, she relates both true and fictional stories about her Lowcountry present and world-traveling past. Writing offers her a lens to view the world, and a strategy to thrive within its madness. She straddles both through a non-fiction series she calls *Life in Third Person* and the poetry of *Silk Purses and Lemonade*. "Life in the Pink Palace" chronicles in prose a week she spent in an ICU waiting room hoping her son would survive. He did. "Beware of Flying Pigs" navigates similar emotions in a poem. While many find faith carries them, Robin pins hope to compassion, sheer will, and the integrity in acceptance.

Her work appears in *The Fourth River, Foliate Oak Literary Magazine, I am not a silent poet, Autumn Sky Poetry Daily, Curly Mind, The Skinny Journal* and locally in *The Breeze* and the Island Writers' Network's *Time and Tide*.

See more at www.elizabethrobin.com.

www.ingramcontent.com/pod-product-compliance
Lightning Source LLC
LaVergne TN
LVHW041508070426
835507LV00012B/1416